THE FAMILY TREE

GROWING A GODLY FAMILY

by Dr. Randy T. Johnson
WITH CONTRIBUTIONS BY:

NOBLE BAIRD
JAMES CLOUSE
ISAIAH COMBS
JAYSON COMBS
JEN COMBS
JOSHUA COMBS
SIERRA COMBS
JEFF ENGLAND
DONNA FOX
RICHIE HENSON
DEBBIE KERR

CHUCK LINDSEY
JAMES MANN
WES MCCULLOUGH
MARK O'CONNOR
PHIL PIASECKI
MAX SINCLAIR
RYAN STORY
KYLE WENDEL
KATRINA YOUNG
TOMMY YOUNGQUIST

DESIGN BY: CASEY MAXWELL

Copyright © 2018 The River Church

All rights reserved. No part of this book may be reproduced or transmitted in any form or by any means, electronic or mechanical, including photocopying, recording or by any information storage and retrieval system, without the written permission of The River Church. Inquiries should be sent to the publisher.

First Edition, January 2018

Published by:
The River Church
8393 E. Holly Rd.
Holly, MI 48442

Scriptures are taken from the Bible,
English Standard Version (ESV)

THE RIVER CHURCH

Printed in the United States of America

CONTENTS

WEEK 1

PLANTING

09	Study Guide
15	Devotion 1: GPS
17	Devotion 2: Directions
19	Devotion 3: Fig Tree
21	Devotion 4: Unicycle Toward Him
23	Devotion 5: Abide
25	Devotion 6: Train Up a Child

WEEK 2

NURTURING

29	Study Guide
35	Devotion 1: Thanks Mom
37	Devotion 2: The Power of Forgiveness
39	Devotion 3: Teachable Moments
41	Devotion 4: Power of the Spoken Word
43	Devotion 5: Leave a Mark
45	Devotion 6: Husband and Wife

WEEK 3

PRUNING

49	Study Guide
61	Devotion 1: Shears Energy
63	Devotion 2: Tough to Love When You Favor
65	Devotion 3: Bait and Switch
69	Devotion 4: That Crazy Uncle
71	Devotion 5: Forgiveness
73	Devotion 6: Discipline

WEEK 4

BLOOMING

79	Study Guide
89	Devotion 1: Love
91	Devotion 2: Joy
93	Devotion 3: Peace
95	Devotion 4: Patience
97	Devotion 5: Kindness
99	Devotion 6: Goodness
101	Devotion 7: Faithfulness
105	Devotion 8: Gentleness
107	Devotion 9: Self-Control

PREFACE

Your family is God-given.

Does that phrase bring a smile or grimace to your face?
How can we enjoy our family more?
How can we help our family reach its full potential?
How can the topics of planting, nurturing, pruning, and blooming relate to the family?
Are there times and ways we might need to distance ourselves from negative family influences?

Psalm chapter 1 gives a beautiful balance of the Christian walk having proper relationships horizontally and of course vertically. God placed us in our family. It is not always easy or healthy. How we interact affects our walk. Verse two shows how God's Word is a catalyst for development. The result paints a beautiful picture of our family tree:

"He is like a tree planted by streams of water that yields its fruit in its season, and its leaf does not wither. In all that he does, he prospers." Psalm 1:3

The Family Tree consists of four study guides for personal or group discussion and twenty-seven devotions to help you and your family flourish, prosper, and blossom.

01
PLANTING

**CHUCK LINDSEY,
REACH PASTOR**

PLANTING WEEK 1

Dandelions. They are the enemy of all suburban lawns everywhere! While they can be pretty in their yellow flowering stage, they soon turn to those evil little "puff balls" of seeds that fly all over the place infiltrating every nearby and unsuspecting lawn. Nothing says, "I do not have time for lawn care" like a yard full of dandelions.

Have you ever struggled with weeds in your lawn or garden? What did you do to get rid of them? _____

_____

_____

Did you know that weeds, like dandelions, actually prefer bad ground? It is true. In my research for how to get rid of them, I found that many varieties of weeds prefer ground that is dry, shallow, and lacking nutrients. It is so interesting that most weeds thrive in the exact opposite kind of ground that is needed to grow good plants and fruit trees. As I researched, I immediately realized the spiritual implications.

The same is true in our own lives and families. Good fruit grows in good soil, but weeds and thorns grow in bad soil. The "weeds" of sin, pride, selfishness, anger, bitterness, lust, discontentment, and complaining all grow and become strong in the heart and life of a person whose "soil" (life) is spiritually dry and empty. As a pastor, I see it all the time. When a person's life is void of the life giving "ground" of Jesus and the "nutrients" of His Word, weeds are everywhere! When a person's life is shallow and self-focused, their lives are also full of the weeds of sin and the thorns that come with them. That is just the way it is.

Now, it would be unrealistic to plant fruit trees in such soil expecting good fruit to grow. That is what many people and families are trying

John 15:4

9

PLANTING WEEK 1

to do. Many are not spiritually careful. They allow all kinds of ungodly things (weeds) into their lives and families.

Can you think of some "weeds" people allow into their lives? ____
_____
_____

These things cause damage and hurt (they always have thorns) and yet, many times they still want the good fruit of God's blessings.

Give some examples of the kinds of "good fruit" people want in their lives. _____
_____
_____

They truly want peace, joy, hope, and purpose in their lives and families. However, they are trying to get good fruit to grow in bad soil. Soil like that will never produce good fruit. It just does not work.

The truth is (to continue stretching the metaphor), everyone is planted in some kind of "soil." Like plants or trees, we are all drawing what we need from the soil in which we are planted. Think about that for a moment.

In what kind of soil are you planted? _____
_____
_____

If we are planted in the soil that is Jesus, then we are planted in soil that is deep, well-watered, and rich with the nutrients needed for life. The result is that good fruit can grow. But if we are planted in any other soil, we will be drawing what we need from that which cannot produce life. Jesus is life (John 1:4), and only He can give us

Matthew 13
sower

life. Only Jesus is good and can produce good things and fruit in us. Jesus said it this way:

> *"Abide in Me, and I in you. As the branch cannot bear fruit of itself, unless it abides in the vine, neither can you, unless you abide in Me.*
>
> *'I am the vine, you are the branches. He who abides in Me, and I in him, bears much fruit; for without Me you can do nothing.'" (John 15:4-5 NKJV)*

Psalm 1:1-3 (NKJV) says something very similar:

> *"Blessed is the man*
> *Who walks not in the counsel of the ungodly,*
> *Nor stands in the path of sinners,*
> *Nor sits in the seat of the scornful;*
> *But his delight is in the law of the Lord,*
> *And in His law he meditates day and night.*
> *He shall be like a tree*
> *Planted by the rivers of water,*
> *That brings forth its fruit in its season,*
> *Whose leaf also shall not wither;*
> *And whatever he does shall prosper."*

There it is, when we are planted in the Lord and His Word, we are like trees that are planted near water, and good fruit grows in our lives.

Describe some of the good fruit that comes from being planted in the Lord and His Word. _____
_____
_____

PLANTING WEEK 1

Now, as we bring this to a close, it might be obvious to hear it, but the way to get rid of the weeds in our lives, or our families is the same way you get rid of weeds in your lawn. You have to fix your soil! That means that if you are already a follower of Jesus Christ, then it is time to pull some weeds! That is right, there comes the point when you just need to pull weeds. For good fruit to begin to grow again, we are going to need to fix the soil of our lives and homes. The first step is to ask God for His forgiveness for the way that things have become. Then start pulling weeds. Pour out, turn off, and throw out whatever is tripping you up. These two things together (asking God for forgiveness and pulling weeds) is called "repentance." Repentance is an essential step that is like a rototiller breaking up the ground of our hearts, making it ready to receive good seed. Next, we have to start planting good seed again. That comes from the Bible. It is the seed of God's Word. It is not books about God. It is God's Word, the Bible. A steady diet of God's Word is all the difference! As we both hear and do what God says, good growth begins to happen. It is called discipleship. Lastly, we must be careful to watch for weeds that want to spring up again. Sin, like weeds, are always right there, wanting to grow again in your life. As a kid pulling weeds, I found the small ones were always the easiest to pull. The difficult ones were the ones that grew large. So when we see these weeds beginning to grow again, it is time to pull them, but do it when they are small!

Why do you think it is important to pull weeds when they are small rather than when they are full grown? _____
_____
_____

Next, we do those things that promote good growth.

PLANTING WEEK 1

Being a part of weekly gatherings is like watering the plants! How?

_____

_____

Being a part of a weekly Growth Community is like adding miracle grow to the soil! How?

_____

_____

Finally, as we reach out to others about what Jesus has done for them, we start to see this orchard grow! It is thrilling. How so?

_____

_____

_____

Now, there might be someone reading this who does not yet have a relationship with the Lord. Your life is full of the weeds we have been talking about, and you do not know where to start. Is that you? Listen, Jesus is the answer. You need to be planted in Him. As we said before, He is the only soil that a person can be planted in that produces life. So, the only way for your kids to bear good fruit is for them to come to Jesus, confessing their sin, and receiving Him as Lord. If they do, they will be planted in Him. The same is true for you. As we see our need (lives full of weeds and thorns), and we look to Him, repenting of our sin (which means to turn from it and turn to Him), and we ask Him to become the Lord of our lives, the Bible promises that He will forgive our sins and make us His own. That is when good fruit begins!

GPS

PLANTING, DEVOTION 1
Wes McCullough | *Production Director*

God's
Perfect
Steering

The world used to get navigation instructions from an atlas or word of mouth. Reading an atlas was a learned skill, and some people gave bad directions, so you did not always get where you wanted to go easily. Today we all use GPS and know exactly where we are and the fastest route to where we are headed. I find myself no longer paying attention when someone gives me verbal directions knowing I will type in the address and GPS will direct me turn by turn.

Jeremiah 17:5-6 gives us wisdom on who we should trust as we navigate this world.

> *"Thus says the Lord:*
> *'Cursed is the man who trusts in man*
> *and makes flesh his strength,*
> *whose heart turns away from the Lord.*
> *He is like a shrub in the desert,*
> *and shall not see any good come.*
> *He shall dwell in the parched places of the wilderness,*
> *in an uninhabited salt land.'"*

The Bible is clear that those who trust in men will not prosper. Like a thirsty plant in the desert, they will always be unsatisfied and searching for what is not there. We have all learned the life lesson that people will let you down because man is fallible. Whether by mistake or incompetence we have faced disappointment when trusting in man. The passage continues with good advice.

"Blessed is the man who trusts in the Lord,
whose trust is the Lord.
He is like a tree planted by water,
that sends out its roots by the stream,
and does not fear when heat comes,
for its leaves remain green,
and is not anxious in the year of drought,
for it does not cease to bear fruit."

God is the best navigator, of course, because he knows everything. God's promise in these verses is beautiful; trust in the Lord and when hard times come there will be no worry. When you are rooted in the Heavenly Father, trials do not mean the end. God sustains us through hard times so incredibly that we come through having prospered.

Life is a journey that takes you over new, perfectly smooth roads and old roads with deep pot holes. When you trust in God and follow His navigation, you not only get where you need to go, but you arrive in better condition than you left.

DIRECTIONS

PLANTING, DEVOTION 2
Isaiah Combs | *Worship Leader and Young Adults Director*

I am awful at directions. I get lost on almost a daily basis (ask my wife). My phone could be giving me directions, and I still manage to get lost. I cannot tell you how many times the hour trip to the airport has turned into a three to four-hour excursion. It is not just road directions either. Written directions on how to build something are also a struggle.

I think once a year my wife likes to torture me by making me drive her to the place where dreams go to die. It is a man's worst nightmare. It is IKEA (said with an evil chill-down-your-back tone).

There are two reasons I loath IKEA:
1. Driving there and back (usually with something way too big that should not go into your car).
2. Knowing I have to go home and put it together with the quote on it saying, "easy directions."

It always takes me way longer than it is supposed to put things together. I usually take a break and walk around because I am typically angry and am contemplating if the money spent on the item is worth me breaking it apart with a sledge hammer (Hi, my name is Isaiah, and I struggle with anger. But that is for another time, place, or devotion).

I am directionally challenged.

The Bible is full of directions. The Bible contains perfect directions on how to steer your life. Want to know how to build your life? Do you want to know how to build and direct your family?

Psalms 1:1-3 says, *"**Blessed is the man who walks not in the counsel of the wicked, nor stands in the way of sinners, nor sits in the seat of scoffers; but his delight is in the law of the Lord, and on his law he meditates day and night. He is like a tree planted by streams of water that yields its fruit in its season, and its leaf does not wither. In all that he does, he prospers."***

I need to focus on verse two. Blessed is a man who delights in the Word of the Lord and thinks or reflects on it all day, every day.

I know what you are thinking. It is easier said than done. That may be true, but God gives you some motivation.

Verse 3 is what happens when you follow these directions. All that you do you will prosper. Please grasp this point, ALL THAT YOU DO YOU WILL PROSPER. I just want to make sure you get it.

God's Word and way allows you to prosper and succeed in your marriage, parenting, job, and life in general.

As I said, I am terrible at following directions and getting in the Word. Growing and learning can be hard. However, the Word is very clear on what happens when you do. If you would like to succeed in all you do, the key is to follow the directions given to you by God in the Bible.

FIG TREE

PLANTING, DEVOTION 3
Richie Henson | *Production Director*

Life today can feel so complicated. There are so many responsibilities with places to be and people to see. There are times when I wish life could be more simple. However, when I take a moment to slow down and dwell on the important things in life, I quickly realize all of the over-complicating in life is my own doing. No one is forcing me to be as busy as I am, that is a decision I am making.

In Luke chapter 13, Jesus is speaking to a group of people, and they are trying to complicate the simple truth of repentance. The people were trying to establish a hierarchy of sinners, meaning some people are worse sinners than others and Jesus responds by declaring all people are equal in sin and thereby are equally in need of repentance (Luke 13:1-5). So, to illustrate the simplicity of His point, Jesus tells of a fig tree. This fig tree has not borne fruit for three years. The master is angry with the tree and seeks to cut it down; however, the vineyard keeper desires to add fertilizer to the soil and give it one more year to see if it will bear fruit.

We are all like fig trees, planted in this world with the sole purpose of bearing fruit. However, I think there are times when the idea of bearing fruit becomes convoluted, and we struggle to grasp the simplicity of it.

If we think of the fig tree, we may conclude that the only mandatory requirement for success is bearing fruit. So, we can say that bearing fruit is a direct reference to the fulfillment of a requirement. In our case, as Christians, bearing fruit is the fulfillment of the requirements of God. In Luke chapter 13, Jesus is specifically referencing the requirement of repentance; however, this truth is easily applicable to all of God's directives in our lives.

God has given us clear directives throughout the Bible. As people saved by grace through the blood and resurrection of Jesus, we are filled with the Holy Spirit, thereby, we have received power to move past our human limitations and bear spiritual fruit such as repentance. This idea also means we can live with the Fruit of the Spirit as laid out in Galatians 5:22-23.

As parents and family members, we are only capable of succeeding if we are committed to bearing fruit. That means we must commit to living a Spirit led life as we seek what is holy and acceptable to God. If we commit ourselves to bearing fruit, that is, to fulfill the clear directives of God each day by the power of the Spirit, we can be assured that God, our Master, will be happy with us, His fig tree.

UNICYCLE TOWARD HIM

PLANTING, DEVOTION 4
Phil Piasecki | *Worship Leader*

I have always found it interesting how different families each have their own "thing." What I mean by this is so many families can be identified by what their interests are. I think of families who all work in the same industry, are interested in sports, or are interested in music. Normally, what mom or dad like to do and enjoy gets passed down to their children, and so on and so forth. My dad learned how to ride a unicycle when he was growing up, and when I was old enough, he taught me how to ride it. I highly doubt I would have ever decided on my own to learn how to do that, but it was something that my dad (hilariously) passed down to me. This truth has been so much more evident to me since my wife and I had our first child. Between a year and fifteen months, she started to imitate everything that we did. She would raise her hands in worship when any song came on, and she would imitate our movements when we took her to the gym. The things that we abide in are what our lives reflect, which is why Jesus gives us this command in John 15.

> John 15:4-5 says, ***"Abide in me, and I in you. As the branch cannot bear fruit by itself, unless it abides in the vine, neither can you, unless you abide in me. I am the vine; you are the branches. Whoever abides in me and I in him, he it is that bears much fruit, for apart from me you can do nothing."***

Jesus commands us to abide in Him and warns us that apart from Him we can do nothing. If you think of any fruit tree, when a branch is cut off from the tree it will no longer produce fruit. We are the same as that tree. When we bear fruit, it means that we are becoming more and more like Christ. A family that abides in Christ together will become more like Him. When I picture a family abiding in Christ, I see a family that reads their Bibles together, attends weekly church gatherings together, and serves Christ together. In twenty years, I do not want my family to be known as a sports family, a music family, or a unicycle riding family! I want us to be known as a Jesus family, a family that spent their time abiding in Christ and bore fruit because of it.

A branch abiding in a vine will bear fruit, there is no question about that. We can be confident that if our family is resting in Christ, we will become more like Him. We must constantly be connected to Christ; it cannot be an occasional thing. A branch cannot disconnect from the vine for a period of time, then reattach, and expect to be producing fruit. Christ needs to be the cornerstone of your family. When we abide in Him, we will become more like Christ.

ABIDE

PLANTING, DEVOTION 5
Ryan Story | *Student Pastor*

I had to accept something awhile ago, "I am a family man." By that I mean I have a wife and two sons. To those who knew me in my young adult phase you know this to be true, I never thought I was going to get married let alone have kids. I accepted my fate the moment I said "I do" and I have acted accordingly. From the moment my wife told me she was pregnant, I accepted my fate. In those moments, I knew I would not leave my family; I would remain even through the toughest of times. I would always abide with my family.

In John 15:1-11, Jesus explains that He is the True Vine. Repeatedly, Jesus says, ***"abide in me."*** Simply put the word "abide" means "to stay with." There are two major ways I look at this section of Scripture. The first is how our lives look when we abide with Jesus. To hear Jesus talk about us abiding in Him is comforting like a warm blanket on a cold day. Abiding with Jesus, staying with Jesus, is a decision that never comes back void. It amazes me that people honestly walk away from Him. Take a moment today to think of ways that you can abide more richly in Him.

There needs to be the mega application. When we abide in Jesus fully, we can abide better with those we love. I was able to come to a profound truth recently, if Jesus does not remain my Number One, everything else falls apart. I was told once to think of life like plate spinning. It takes time to get the big plate moving, but once it gets moving you can focus on other plates, and some are larger than others. So if abiding in Jesus is the big plate, then my wife is the next biggest plate, and my sons are the next biggest plate. I have to get the bigger ones going or else, the smaller ones will fall. If I am not focusing on the bigger plate, then I am not focusing on the correct order of plate. Everything will fall. Abiding in Jesus is great because when we fully commit to Him, He seems to help elevate every other area. Who knew making my wife #2 and Jesus my #1 would be the best thing for our marriage?

I truly enjoy my walk with God and enjoy the adventure I am on with my family. There are few things in my life that bring me genuine joy. Jesus and my family are the two at the top of my list. I mess up, and at times I feel like a sub-par husband and a below average father. But that does not stop me from figuring out what I need to do to change that. The issue always seems to be when I start walking away from God. Abiding with God for the sake of my family seems to be the one thing that always seems to fix the issues. What are the things that bring you true joy? If they are found in God, how can growing closer to God help you grow in your joy?

TRAIN UP A CHILD

PLANTING, DEVOTION 6
Sierra Combs | *Women's Ministry Director*

"Train up a child in the way he should go; even when he is old he will not depart from it." Proverbs 22:6

If you are a Bible reading person who has ever raised a child, I can almost guarantee that you have heard this verse. Perhaps you have it memorized or painted on signs in your home. Some of you might quote it daily or if you are extreme maybe even have it tattooed on your arm so that you can be reminded of it at all times. Why? Because raising children is hard work. It is gut wrenchingly hard work. Sure, kids are amazing. The joys and rewards of raising them are pretty unbeatable. But it is hard! While being a parent is one of the greatest blessings God has given us, it is also one of our greatest responsibilities.

"Train up a child in the way he should go." What does this mean? According to the dictionary, to train means "to develop or form the habits, thoughts, or behavior by discipline and instruction." I think of Olympic level athletes and how they got to their level of success. They were not just born superstars, they had to go through years and even decades of hard work and training to reach their goals. Training is an important and necessary part of life, and it is more than just teaching. When we train our kids, we are molding and shaping their hearts into who we intend them to be, and we are called to start doing that from the very beginning. So how can and how should we train our children? I first should note that even when we are not intentionally training our children, they are still being trained. For example, by failing to discipline them, we teach them that they can

get away with doing whatever they want. By failing to teach them God's Word, they learn that what God says is not that important. That is not good training!

We need to actively and intentionally dedicate the time and care into training up our children in the "way" they should go. What is the way? Better yet, Who is the way? In John 14:6 Jesus tells us that He is *"the way, and the truth, and the life."* Teaching our children about Jesus and showing them how to live godly lives is the best kind of training we can give our kids. Even Moses stressed the importance of teaching God's commandments when he told the Israelites to *"repeat them again and again to your children. Talk about them when you are at home and when you are on the road, when you are going to bed and when you are getting up. Tie them to your hands and wear them on your forehead as reminders. Write them on the doorposts of your house and on your gates"* (Deuteronomy 6:7-9 NLT). If we want our children to follow God, we must live our lives with Him at the very center and as the focus. I encourage you to be in the Word with your children. Pray with them, talk about what God wants to do in their lives. God has given you an extremely important role and responsibility! Do not waste it!

The second half of the verse is probably the part that people want to cling to the most. *"Train up a child in the way he should go; even when he is old he will not depart from it."* The second half of this verse is the part that makes a lot of people feel good and safe. But as much as I wish this were an absolute promise and perfect formula given by God, it is not a foolproof plan. Like the rest of the Proverbs, this is just another general truth written by a wise man. The fact is that while we will be held accountable to God for what we do or do not do in the early years of our children's lives, eventually that responsibility shifts over to them. As a mom, I want nothing more than to see my kids become godly individuals who make great choices and do incredible things for God. We can train them, teach them, pray for them, and hope beyond hopes that they become these people, but we cannot make that happen. That is up to them. In the meantime, let us continue to be heart shapers, teaching and training our children in the way of the Lord and giving thanks to the Father for passionately pursuing them every single day.

02
NURTURING

JAYSON COMBS,
FAMILY PASTOR

NURTURING WEEK 2

Disclaimer: Before we start, it is important to mention the significance of this lesson for both those with children and those who do not have children. All of us are called to impact and love people, whether they are our children in the home, nieces and nephews, friends, or colleagues. The Bible is very clear that the older women are called to teach the younger, and it is the same for the men. So, as we dig deep, please reflect on the people God has placed in your life.

How can you nurture them and help them grow in their walk with Christ? _____
_____
_____

One of the worst things in the world for a Youth Pastor is the dreaded all-nighter. It is the event where middle school and high school kids get to hang out and stay awake all night. Unfortunately, the leaders must do the same. Many years ago, I was a middle school Youth Director, and we had one of these "horrific" events in which over one hundred students decided to push through the entire night for fun. I had rented out a community center with a pool, gym, and inflatables. As the night went on, I began to receive complaints from some of the girls. One after another reports were made that bags in the girl's locker room had been opened and gone through and that several items were missing. At the end of the event, I brought all the girls into a room and told them that we had a thief and that throughout the night someone had been stealing money, jewelry, and whatever else they could find that was valuable. I told the girls that I had contacted the local Police Department and a Police Officer was waiting upstairs. I also made it clear to the girls that they could either tell me and be done with it, or tell the cop (a pretty good play by me if I do say so myself).

Immediately, four girls start pointing at each other. Each one said the other one made them do it. I had the girls return the items and then the best part happened; I went home to sleep. I got up early that afternoon and contacted the parents of the girls who had taken the items. As a young Youth Pastor, I think it was one of the most shocking conversations I had ever had. One of the moms was mad at me. She stated "girls would be girls" and that I had "completely overreacted." It seemed like the mom saw this as normal behavior for middle schoolers and that I needed to stop bullying her daughter. From this conversation, I realized the family structure, in many cases, was and still is very broken.

> Paul, in Ephesians 6:4, tells us how to nurture and grow the family in the way of the Lord, ***"Fathers, do not provoke your children to anger, but bring them up in the discipline and instruction of the Lord."***

> Deuteronomy 6:7 adds, ***"You shall teach them diligently to your children, and shall talk of them when you sit in your house, and when you walk by the way, and when you lie down, and when you rise."***

In Ephesians 6, the word "father" is translated from the Greek word "*pateres.*" In the book of Hebrews, however, the same Greek word is translated as "parents." There does seem to be an emphasis on the "father" in the Ephesians passage, but I believe the following principles can be applied to both the father and mother.

So what does this verse in Ephesians tell us as parents? Paul gives three actions for nurturing children that we will focus on for this lesson: bring, discipline, and instruct.

The first action comes from the word *"bring."* Other translations translate it "nurture." The same word is used in Ephesians 5:29, ***"For no one ever hated his own flesh, but nourishes and cherishes it, just as Christ does the church."***

Can you remember a time in your life when your parents brought you to something and totally embarrassed you? _____
_____
_____

There is a discussion among many church leaders across the globe as to who should be teaching the children. For decades now, the church has created a divided learning structure where kids and adults have separate classes and gathering times. Some churches, however, are moving toward a more joint teaching and learning time. This argument seems to support the call in the Bible for parents to *bring* up their children in the Lord. Many supporters of this argument also feel the church has failed the family because the church has facilitated the convenience of sending instead of bringing. Personally, I do see a lot of validity in this argument. Too many times, parents want to send their kids to be taught instead of realizing their role as parents to *bring* their kids along in their walk with Jesus. However, it must be noted that I also believe the church has a very significant role in *helping* parents teach their kids.

What are some practical ways in which we can bring our children along with us in our walk with Christ? _____
_____
_____

What struggles do you have in doing this? _____
_____
_____

The second action for fathers or parents is to *discipline*. wThe beginning of Ephesians 6:4 gives a warning, **"To not provoke your children to anger."** Colossians 3:21 elaborates upon the warning by stating, **"Fathers, do not provoke your children, lest they become discouraged."** In my experience, this anger and discouragement in sons and daughters can be a direct result of parents who do not know how to properly discipline. Warren Wiersbe, an American Pastor and author, states:

"Parents provoke their children and discourage them by saying one thing and doing another—by always blaming and never praising. By being inconsistent and unfair in discipline and by showing favoritism in the home by making promises and not keeping them and by making light of problems that to the children are very important. Christian parents need the fullness of the Spirit so they can be sensitive to the needs and problems of their children."

What things do you do to provoke your children to anger? _____
_____
_____

The word 'discipline' from the Ephesians passage can also be translated 'to train,' indicating the need to steer and protect your children. It seems parents do not understand the importance of protecting their kids from things such as phones, computers, friends, and dating relationships.

How does a parents' protection of their child change as their son or daughter grows from an infant to a child, a child to a teenager, and a teenage to an adult? _____
_____
_____

NURTURING WEEK 2

What areas do you struggle with when it comes to discipline and/or protection? _____
_____
_____

The last action for parents to consider is *instructing* their children, which can also be translated "to put in the mind."

Who was the best instructor you have ever had? Why did that instructor have such an impact in your life? _____
_____
_____

What is going to make you a better instructor when it comes to raising your children? Romans 16:19 can help, **"But I want you to be wise as to what is good and innocent as to what is evil."**

What are things that you have found to be effective when it comes to instructing your children? _____
_____
_____

Who is one person in your life the group can pray for that you would like to help nurture? _____
_____
_____

THANKS MOM

NURTURING, DEVOTION 1
Debbie Kerr | *Office Administrator*

"And, ye fathers, provoke not your children to wrath: but bring them up in the nurture and admonition of the Lord."
(Ephesians 6:4 KJV)

When I think of the word nurture regarding parenting my mind immediately thinks of mothers. Nurturing comes naturally to women and traditionally, mothers spend the most time with the children. My mom still nurtures me even in the latter stages of Alzheimer's. I am not sure she is even aware of it, but it is her nature as my mother. Growing up, my mom was the disciplinarian, and my dad was the fun parent. He would never allow my mom to "hold off" disciplining or say "wait until your father gets home!" He did not want his daughters to dread his homecoming. My mother was perfectly suited to be the disciplinarian and did it like a boss, but my dad knew how to nurture and admonish as well. He would step in when needed, but she pretty much got the job done! Regardless of who did the disciplining, they always made sure we knew we were intensely loved before we were dismissed. None of us rebelled because their discipline was wrapped in a huge soft blanket of unconditional love, with the addition of a godly teachable moment. Otherwise, it is known as nurture and admonition in perfect harmony.

By definition "to nurture" means many things. The *Webster's Dictionary's* list includes: To train, nourish, care for, educate, encourage, support, nurse, comfort and cultivate, just to name a few. God gives us eighteen plus years to accomplish this as parents. It is nurture that takes a baby completely dependent on us into independent adulthood.

So, what does nurturing in the Lord look like? In Deuteronomy 6:7-9 God described to Moses, the Patriarch, what it looks like to raise a child in the nurture and admonition of the Lord. He told Moses, ***"You shall teach them (the law and statutes of the Lord) diligently to your children, and you shall talk of them when you sit in your house and when walk by the way, when you lie down, and when you rise. You shall bind them as a sign on your hand, and they shall be as frontlets between our eyes. You shall write them on the doorposts of your house and on your gates."*** God wanted Moses and the Israelites to know that living a life of God's principles is a 24/7 thing. It is not just reserved for an hour on Sunday morning; it must be consistent and a part of everything we say and do. What children learn and see modeled in the home will often outweigh all other influences. You cannot depend on the church solely to raise your children, but they will be a huge support and add to your efforts.

A great verse of encouragement given to parents is Proverbs 22:6, ***"Train up a child in the way he should go: and when he is old, he will not depart from it."*** There is no such thing as a perfect parent, we fail and make mistakes. However, when we follow God's blueprint for parenting, we will have a higher spiritual success rate. Parenting is one of the highest callings a person can receive. It is long, amazing, exhausting, exuberant, exhausting, blissful, exhausting; you get my point! Parents and grandparents, we have an amazing opportunity to help nurture and shape the next generation to the glory of God. It is a priceless investment that yields an eternal return!

THE POWER OF FORGIVENESS

NURTURING, DEVOTION 2
Ryan Story | *Student Pastor*

I worked in Head Start for a few years when I was going for my Associates Degree. Head Start is a program for low economic pre-school aged students that helps them get a "head start" when they start Kindergarten. Attending a few meetings, I heard several times that "education is the only thing that can break the cycle of poverty." Head Start's mission, so to speak, was to help kids out of poverty in their lives; they had to get through grade school and college to get a good job to not repeat the trend. I loved working with this program and loved working in the classrooms I had. Agree or disagree with their view, the idea that adding one element can stop a cycle of destruction is an amazing thought. If you look in your life, go back to a point when you added Jesus' forgiveness into the cycle of life you were living. Did it change everything? Of course, adding Jesus to anyone's life can change the way a person lives, but there is much power in us forgiving others.

Take some time this week to read about Joseph in Genesis chapters 38-50. With all of the stuff that Joseph had to endure because of his brothers, and slightly his pride, Joseph had an opportunity to destroy his brothers, but he chose to forgive them and embrace them. Even after Jacob had died the book of Genesis (chapter 50) says:

> *"Say to Joseph, 'Please forgive the transgression of your brothers and their sin, because they did evil to you. And now, please forgive the transgression of the servants of the God of your father.' Joseph wept when they spoke to him. His brothers also came and fell down before him and said,*

'Behold, we are your servants.' But Joseph said to them, 'Do not fear, for am I in the place of God? As for you, you meant evil against me, but God meant it for good, to bring it about that many people should be kept alive, as they are today. So do not fear; I will provide for you and your little ones.' Thus he comforted them and spoke kindly to them" (verses 17-21).

Joseph's brothers knew they had done wrong, and were fearful of what would happen after Jacob's death. God was able to move Joseph to a place where he realized that everything that happens is because of God, the good and the bad. Forgiveness in the family is hard because the hurt is closer. If you are struggling with forgiveness, think about the cycle you can break by forgiving the person who has hurt you. It becomes so easy for us to not move forward because "you do not know what that person did to me" or "you do not know how much that hurt." But the cycles of bitterness, revenge, insecurities, hostility, and resentment must end so we can move closer to what God has for us. I understand that these words are easier to type than to live out, but from someone who has battled with forgiving those in my life who have hurt me, it is amazing what God has for us on the other side.

TEACHABLE MOMENTS

NURTURING, DEVOTION 3
Phil Piasecki | *Worship Leader*

I have some of the largest oak trees around my house that I have ever seen in the state of Michigan. There are three of them in my front yard and every fall they dump what seems like a million leaves on my yard. I do my best to clean them all up, but every year since I bought the house I have left a small pile of leaves somewhere in my yard, and it kills all the grass underneath it. So in the Spring, I get grass seed, spread it over the dead part, water it, and see the grass come to life again. If I did not water those grass seeds, I would be left with a dead patch of soil. Spreading that seed is not enough, it needs to be watered. The same is true for our families. When the seed of salvation is planted in the hearts of our kids, spouse, or even ourselves, that seed needs to be watered with the teachings of Christ.

> Deuteronomy 6:4-9 says, *"Hear, O Israel: The Lord our God, the Lord is one. You shall love the Lord your God with all your heart and with all your soul and with all your might. And these words that I command you today shall be on your heart. You shall teach them diligently to your children, and shall talk of them when you sit in your house, and when you walk by the way, and when you lie down, and when you rise. You shall bind them as a sign on your hand, and they shall be as frontlets between your eyes. You shall write them on the doorposts of your house and on your gates."*

This Scripture lays out such an incredible picture of what it looks like to have a family that is being nurtured in the things of Christ. First, it instructs us to love God with all our heart, soul, and might. If you are a believer, it should be your desire to love and seek God with everything you have inside of you. Think of an athlete training to be the best at their sport; they go after it every day. We, in the same way, need to seek the things of Christ every day. If we do not water our spiritual life, it will never grow! The Scripture continues, showing us how we can nurture and water our kid's walk with Christ. It says we are to talk about God's commandments when we walk, lie down, and get up. What this Scripture is practically telling us is that we should take every opportunity that we have to point what happens in our lives towards Christ. There are so many incredible teaching opportunities every day, and we so often miss them. Do the right thing, and then explain to your kids the biblical reason behind why you did what you did. Love your crazy neighbor, and then explain to your kids that we love that person because Jesus first loved us. The things of Christ should not be something that is only talked about on Sunday. If you are relying on a Pastor to water your children's spiritual life you are going to be disappointed. It is the responsibility of the family to constantly be pointing each other towards the things of Christ. Kids, you can reflect Jesus to your parents every day as well. Talk about Jesus with them, take the opportunities in your everyday life to point back to Christ. Jesus needs to be at the forefront of our minds. A family pushing each other towards Christ will see their relationship with Him grow exponentially.

POWER OF THE SPOKEN WORD

NURTURING, DEVOTION 4
Noble Baird | *Community Center Director*

Every year on Thanksgiving, my aunt, uncle, and cousin come to my parent's house for dinner. It has become sort of a tradition for us as a family, one that I look forward to every year. Several years ago, when I was in college at Moody, I came home over Thanksgiving break and like every year before, I was excited to spend time with family. However, this year was a bit different. Coming home during my second year of Bible School, I thought this might be the right opportunity to talk to my cousin about going to church and living "right." As the day progressed and we hung out, I had time hanging with my cousin in the basement and thought this might be the chance. The way in which I tried to talk and convey church and God's Word to him was not very tactful and came across, to him, as if I was attacking him. Sadly, things turned sour and ended with him telling me how he respects what I do and why I am going to college, but not to interfere with his life and decisions.

The power of our words and speech are, at times, beyond our comprehension. With mere words, Hitler led an army to cause one of the greatest acts of hate our world will ever see. With two simple words "I do" a lifetime of love and adventure begins. In Proverbs 12:18, Solomon reminds us of the very power of our word. He writes, **"There is one whose rash words are like sword thrusts, but the tongue of the wise brings healing."** Solomon, who is undoubtedly one of the wisest men to ever walk this earth, knew how strong our words are. He knew how quickly they could be used to destroy a life, without even using a weapon. He also knew how if used correctly, they could save one's life and provide hope, love, guidance, and healing.

I have never forgotten the words my cousin said to me and how I had accidentally offended him so much with my words. It was not what I meant or wanted to do at all. As the years have passed and God has opened doors for reconciliation, my cousin and I are closer than ever. We have become so close that he stood by my side the day that I was privileged to say the words "I do" to the love of my life. Not only has God given me a chance to reconcile from that day years ago, but He has given me the chance to lovingly speak truth into my cousin's life. I continually pray for my cousin, because I do not want him to go through this life without knowing the love of Christ and the blessing that comes from being called His.

So, as we continue in our family series, I challenge you to think of that family member who is in need of Christ's love. Maybe you too have had an experience like mine where your words came across strong and not at all how you planned. As you prayerfully ask God for an opportunity to speak love and truth into that family member's life, never give up and remember the words of Solomon on how powerful our words truly are!

LEAVE A MARK

NURTURING, DEVOTION 5
Wes McCullough | *Production Director*

Social media is a great thing. No longer is lengthy and intermittent written correspondence needed to keep up with the lives of friends, loved ones, and others. Now we are always connected to those people through websites and apps.

As much as social media can bring people together, it can also drive them apart. The days of 8-year-olds saying to friends, "You cannot come to my birthday!" because of a disagreement are gone. No longer do middle school girls have to say, "You are not my friend anymore." Today those actions are accomplished with the simple task of "unfriending" someone on social media sites. It has happened a few times to me. Even more shocking has been seeing family members "unfriend" each other. My policy is not to "unfriend" anyone. In my mind, despite whatever situation or disagreement we have had, I still care about and want the best for them.

Paul was a relentless apostle throughout the New Testament books. His life was dedicated to taking the Gospel to all the world. In Acts, we read about a mission trip Paul took with Barnabas and John Mark, where John Mark left them before their trip was finished. John Mark's premature departure would cause problems on later trips.

> *"And after some days Paul said to Barnabas, 'Let us return and visit the brothers in every city where we proclaimed the word of the Lord, and see how they are.' Now Barnabas wanted to take with them John called Mark. But Paul thought best not to take with them one who had withdrawn from them in Pamphylia and had not gone with them to*

the work. And there arose a sharp disagreement, so that they separated from each other. Barnabas took Mark with him and sailed away to Cyprus, but Paul chose Silas and departed, having been commended by the brothers to the grace of the Lord. And he went through Syria and Cilicia, strengthening the churches." (Acts 15:36-41)

What catches my attention in that passage is "sharp." Paul and Barnabas had a passionate disagreement about taking John Mark with them. Paul likely doubted John Mark's dedication to the important task of evangelizing, while Barnabas was looking to give him a second chance. Neither man would compromise on their position. They split ways, and there is no record that they reunited.

Everyone loves second chances and happy endings. Previous sermons and devotions have taught about forgiveness. How many times should we forgive someone? The clear answer is as many times as God forgives us. God does not stop offering second chances and neither should we.

HUSBAND AND WIFE

NURTURING, DEVOTION 6
Dr. Randy T. Johnson | *Growth Pastor*

The Family Tree starts with a couple. When a man and woman get married, they may talk about enlarging the family, but it needs to start with their relationship to each other. Love and respect must be at the core. Nurturing starts with each other. The tendency can be to put all our focus on the children, but the Bible is clear that it needs to start with each other.

Ephesians 5:22-24 says, ***"Wives, submit to your own husbands, as to the Lord. For the husband is the head of the wife even as Christ is the head of the church, his body, and is himself its Savior. Now as the church submits to Christ, so also wives should submit in everything to their husbands."*** The wife is to love her man by respecting him. She needs to be proud of him and express it. He needs to be her number one priority, even before the children.

Before we men start applauding, verse 25 continues the conversation, ***"Husbands, love your wives, as Christ loved the church and gave himself up for her."*** It must be important because in verse 28 Paul repeats the command to husbands, ***"In the same way husbands should love their wives as their own bodies. He who loves his wife loves himself."*** The husband is to love his woman by sacrificing for her. He needs to go out of his way to serve her. She needs to be his number one priority, even before work or the children.

I find the topic of *Love Languages* helpful. I think it is important to figure out what activities and actions speak loudest to our spouse.

The five *Love Languages*:
1. Words of affirmation
2. Acts of service
3. Receiving gifts
4. Quality time
5. Physical touch

My wife and I have found that our Love Languages have changed a little through the years. Where me cleaning the kitchen (acts of service) was so appreciated, kind words reach her heart in a deeper way. Jewelry used to be the golden ticket, but now quality time speaks louder. It is important to discuss how to be better for and with each other.

> Verse 33 summarizes for both husbands and wives, ***"However, let each one of you love his wife as himself, and let the wife see that she respects her husband."***

03
PRUNING

JOSHUA AND JEN COMBS,
LEAD PASTOR AND HIS WIFE

PRUNING WEEK 3

How to set gracious, healthy, and biblical boundaries. Pruning: "to cut away or cut back parts of for better shape or more fruitful growth" (*Webster's Dictionary*).

God prunes His people. According to Hebrews chapter 12, He kindly disciplines us to help shape and mold us into the image of His Son. Quoting Proverbs, the author of Hebrews writes, *"The Lord disciplines the one He loves, and chastises every son who He receives."* God removes habits, behaviors, and even sometimes relationships from our lives so that we can be more fruitful for Him. Interestingly, this is something on which God partners with us.

Hebrews 12:11 says, *"For the moment all discipline seems painful rather than pleasant, but later it yields the peaceful fruit of righteousness to those who have been trained by it."*

Read the verse again substituting the word discipline with pruning (The Greek word for discipline could be translated nurture which would encompass the act of pruning).

What are some behaviors or habits that God has pruned (nurtured or disciplined) out of your life? _____

_____ *farmer knows best*

Without a doubt, the two greatest counseling questions that I get as a pastor, center on forgiveness and strained family relationships. The questions often come to cut back time and contact with a family member or the idea of completely cutting them out of their interaction. Many people have wondered aloud about how and where to set boundaries in their relationships. Countless times I have been asked about how to deal with a mother-in-law who is overbearing concerning her son or new grandchild. A family

John 15:1-8
abide
bears fruit

member who keeps asking for money and promises to pay it back, should I give them more money? A brother or sister, who is currently clean from drug addiction, how often, if at all, should I let them in my house or around my kids? What about past abuse? Neglect? Abandonment? Now that I am a Christian, how often should I spend time with unsaved, extremely worldly family members or longtime friends? I have been asked on how to deal with family gossip and what to do when confidentiality was broken, between what was thought to be best friends. I have also been asked how do deal with neighbors, co-workers, former employees or employers, and the list of questions could go on forever.

Admittedly, I am not a great counselor, but I do love people and feel for their tough relational situations and circumstances. Looking to Scripture, I have often tried to help people set boundaries in their lives.

The goal of this study guide is not to give you ammo to yell at your spouse, in-laws, or siblings, but to help you set gracious, healthy, and most importantly biblical boundaries.

To begin, it is necessary to set some very important biblical rules for ourselves, before we set boundaries for others.
#1 – Speak the truth in love – (Ephesians 4:15)
#2 – Be kind – (Ephesians 4:32)
#3 – Be tenderhearted – (Ephesians 4:32)
#4 – Forgive – (Ephesians 4:32)
#5 – Look to Christ – (Ephesians 4:32)

How have you broken these rules? Or better yet, how have you kept them in tough circumstances? _____
_____
_____

We are going to look specifically at boundaries within the framework of the family. I recognize that it is impossible to deal with every situation and address all the unique and sensitive issues in each circumstance, but we will do our best to give some general guidelines and direction.

Relational Priorities
I often find that in dealing with conflict, bitterness, or unmet expectations within families, the fundamental issue is relational boundaries. We set our relational boundaries based on a biblical understanding of relational priorities. Once we understand the Bible's order of priority in human relationships, we can then set healthy expectations for ourselves and one another. These are the most common relationships that need clarity in the area of prioritizing: marriage, children, parents, and siblings.

> *Marriage*
> **"Therefore a man shall leave his father and his mother and hold fast to his wife, and they shall become one flesh."**
> **Genesis 2:24**

We find this passage multiple times in Scripture, in both the Old and New Testaments. Jesus uses this passage to answer a question about divorce from the hypocritical Pharisees. Later, the Apostle Paul would use this passage to teach the basic principles of marriage and illuminate marriage's testimony of Christ's love for His church (Matthew 19:5 and Ephesians 5:31). This passage of Scripture is the building block on which the entire existence of family rests. What is important for us to see is what the King James translates as the **"leaving"** and **"cleaving"** process. When a man and woman are joined in marriage, regardless of previous marriages, close family connections, or children, their chief human relational priority must become one another. If this does not happen, the marriage is doomed to failure and more than likely divorce. Stated very plainly, in marriage the wife must be the husbands #1 human priority and the husband must be the wife's #1 human priority.

Children
"Children are a heritage from the Lord." Psalm 127:3

Children are a blessing and every child, regardless of circumstances surrounding their birth, is a gift from God. However, we must also recognize the equally biblical truth that children are sinful beings like all other humans. They are intrinsically selfish and self-centered. Many marriages have been destroyed because children did not understand or were not put into their proper place. We live in a society where children are running their homes. Budgets, schedules, and what seems like every facet of home life revolves around their every desire and whim. Children must fundamentally be taught from the time they are born that the world does not revolve around them and neither does the home. Jennifer and I are constantly reminding our children that our marriage comes first and then their needs. We do this very plainly with our older children, but our younger children are taught this principle simply by our unwillingness to let them interrupt a conversation between the two of us. We train them to recognize marriage as the foundation of the home (which rests on Christ) and then their role and place as children. We provide for them physically, emotionally, and spiritually (1 Timothy 5:8) within the frame work of marriage first, and second children. Please do not make the mistake of making your children first on your priority list. This is a lethal mistake to your marriage and will have serious consequences for your child.

Step children are a particularly sensitive issue. Blended families are incredibly complex, but the biblical principles of relational priority remain the same.

Parents

"Therefore a man shall leave his father and his mother and hold fast to his wife." Genesis 2:24

Once again we must reflect on the foundational family verse. Traditionally within the marriage vows is included the phrase ***"forsaking all others."*** Not only that, the father of the bride figuratively and literally gives the bride away. No longer is the father the number one man in this woman's life; the husband takes that place. I have seen many fathers unwilling to relinquish this spot in their now married daughter's heart and subsequently hamper the growth of his son-in-law and daughter's oneness. In the same way, I have seen mothers who are unwilling to remove themselves from the top of their son's life list and to recognize his wife as a higher relational priority. When these situations happen, chaos and gossip are quick to follow. If you have married children, willfully take a back seat to their spouse. Be slow to give your opinion, only do so when asked, and with great caution and wisdom.

The Scripture, again on multiple occasions, says, ***"Honor your father and mother (this is the first commandment with a promise)"*** (Ephesians 6:2). Regardless of whether your mother or mother-in-law is Marie Barone from *Everybody Loves Raymond*, God requires us to honor them. As children, we must obey our parents; however, as adults that command no longer applies. We must honor our parents, whether they are alive or have passed away.

To those who are unmarried adults, honor your parents. Maybe at this point in your life, you live with them. Though for a season that may be best, know that moving out and living on your own may be the best option to prevent unnecessary friction. Your parents will often struggle to see you as an adult and not as a child. Setting a healthy boundary and maintaining peace (Ephesians 4:3) may just be as simple as moving out.

Siblings
"Behold, how good and pleasant it is when brothers dwell in unity." Psalm 133:1

I remember the first time my wife and I hung out with my brothers. Jennifer and I, along with Caleb and Isaiah were planning for a VBS in Detroit. We were working on the sets and different decorations when for some reason by brothers picked up Jennifer and dropped her backside first into a garbage can. They laughed as Jen was essentially folded in half. Jen and I had just started dating, so I did not know how she would react. I hate admitting this, but I did nothing to help her. I watched, as I worked, as Jen wiggled and toppled over the trash can. She brushed herself off, walked over to my extremely unsuspecting brother and put him in a now famous and ruthless headlock. A few seconds later she had dropped one brother to the ground. I was pumped and instantly knew this was the girl for me. She could hold her own against Caleb and Isaiah, who are still, years later, teasing her. But the looming threat of a headlock keeps them at bay.

I love my brothers and have countless, incredible memories with them, but marriage changed our relationship. They are each married now and understand. We love each other, but our marriage covenant with God and our wives trumps brotherhood. Not only does marriage supersede our relationship as brothers, but our role as fathers does as well. For each of us, we have "fallen" dramatically on each other's relationship priority list, and that is a good thing. Whether you are close or not to your brothers or sisters, you must make clear your biblical priorities, which will, in turn, help you establish clear and kind boundaries. Expectations for time, holidays, vacations, nights out, phone calls, and whatever else applies will then be understood. Those boundaries may not be loved or even appreciated, but they will be respected when they are clearly and lovingly communicated.

Two BIG Questions:
Is it ever ok to cut (prune) a family member out of my life? _____
_____
_____

Yes, but not forever. This is a boundary of last resort. *"If possible,"* Paul writes, *"so far as it depends on you, live peaceably with all"* (Romans 12:18). If you have exhausted all your efforts to make peace, then let that person go. This is not a license to speak badly about them, sabotage their life in any way, or harbor feelings of unforgiveness. God's Word is simply saying, if you have done all you can, then that is enough. However, if that person ever seeks to make peace, be ready and waiting. This is a difficult and last option boundary to draw. Do not be quick to cut ties. Be quick to forgive and make peace (Matthew 5:9), if possible.

If I have forgiven somebody who hurt me, do I just let them back in my life? _____
_____
_____

My wife and I have heard some horrific, unspeakable stories of hurt, neglect, abuse, and excruciating pain. At times our hearts just break hearing these stories, and we cannot help but join the hurting in holding on to Jesus. In some cases, years have passed, and the person who was hurt has, through the power of Jesus, been able to forgive and begin the healing process. However, the follow-up question is really important: Do things go back to normal, to the way they were? And therein lies a massive struggle that many people are constantly wrestling. I have forgiven, but do I let this person back into my life? Here are a few questions to ask yourself as you wrestle with this tough and complicated issue.

1. Was this person a partner in sin and wants you to return to your old, sinful life? If so, lovingly prune them from your life. Draw a line in the sand, a boundary. Stay away from them. 2 Thessalonians 3:13-15 says, *"As for you, brothers, do not grow weary in doing good. If anyone does not obey what we say in this letter, take note of that person, and have nothing to do with him, that he may be ashamed. Do not regard him as an enemy, but warn him as a brother."*

2. Are you holding a grudge? Have you become bitter? Are you masking the reality that you are unwilling to forgive? Ephesians 4:31 says, *"Let all bitterness and wrath and anger and clamor and slander be put away from you, along with all malice."*

3. Has this person acknowledged their sin against you, asked forgiveness, and changed their ways? Proverbs 28:13 says, *"Whoever conceals his transgressions will not prosper, but he who confesses and forsakes them will obtain mercy."* If the answer to the previous question is yes, then begin the restoration process. If the answer is no or only a partial yes, then set some loving, personal protection guidelines (emotionally and physically if necessary).

Looking to Jesus
We must look to Jesus to realize that He understands our human condition. He experienced family drama, abandonment by his friends, and emotional struggles. Read the following passages and write down the boundary that Jesus set and with whom.

PRUNING WEEK 3

Luke 2:41-51 _____
_____
_____

Matthew 12:46-50 _____
_____
_____

Matthew 16:21-23 _____
_____
_____

Matthew 26:36-38; 17:1 _____
_____
_____

Jesus' ultimate priority was His relationship with His Heavenly Father, everything followed from there. We ought to be the same. Read Matthew 22:34-40.

Conclusion

When I sat down to write this study guide, my wife sat with me as we talked about the variety of counseling sessions and situations with which we have had to deal. She gave me, what I think is, a brilliant insight. She said three profound words: Wrecked, Wrecking, and Wrecker.

Here is your challenge at the conclusion of this study guide. Using the concept of relational priority, do some serious self-assessment. What have you WRECKED by not setting or respecting boundaries?
_____
_____
_____

PRUNING WEEK 3

Are you WRECKING your marriage or home by not graciously communicating your biblical boundaries to your parents, children, siblings, or someone else? _____
_____
_____

Lastly, who is the WRECKER (A person who is unwilling to respect or acknowledge your biblically drawn boundaries based on Scripture's design of relational priorities)? _____
_____
_____

priority
Lord   prune
spouse
children
family

primary branches
  don't prune does
  tremendous harm.
2. not helpful branches
  lose focus, non essential
3. branch - causes damage
  infecting the tree
  ongoing sin / Rebellion
stops the development

Hebrews 12:11-14 (15.)

SHEARS ENERGY

PRUNING, DEVOTION 1
Jen Combs | *Wife of Lead Pastor Josh Combs*

"I am the true vine, and my father is the vinedresser. Every branch in me that does not bear fruit he takes away, and every branch that does bear fruit he prunes that it may bear more fruit." John 15:1-2

With the convenience of the grocery store, most of us have no idea what goes into growing the fruit that we so nonchalantly throw into our cart. Jesus is talking in these verses, and He is describing some things in a way that everyone during that time would fully understand. It can be explained in such a way that we understand where He is going with this.

Picture an apple tree. I have an apple tree in my garden that is huge and has been there for many, many years. The trunk is large, and if you wanted to get to the top branches, you would need a super tall ladder. I am not sure how tall because I am lazy and I never pick higher than I can reach or that my kids can climb! Like the tree analogy, Jesus calls Himself the vine. Think of Him as the trunk of this apple tree; He is firm and steady. He is holding us up, and we cannot grow without Him. That makes us the branches of the apple tree, but we will get to that in a minute. The vinedresser in the analogy is God. You are probably thinking, "What in the world is a vinedresser?" This is someone who prunes, trains, and cultivates vines.

Every year, if I am on top of things, I look at my apple trees and assess how all of my branches look. I ask several questions. Are

PRUNING DEVOTION 1

there too many shoots growing off of them? Are the shoots sucking the life out of one branch? Are there branches growing over each other choking each other? Are there dead branches that are dried up? If they are any of the above, I need to prune them out for the betterment of the whole tree. If I do not, I hurt the tree, it will be weak, diseased, and not grow great fruit.

Just like the verses say, He prunes and takes away so that it may bear more fruit. This is what God does to our lives. He is pruning us, cultivating us, and training us so we can be more fruitful for the Kingdom of God. Sometimes when I prune the apple tree, it looks so bear that I stand back and gasp thinking, what did I just do? But, low and behold, the next growing season it is beautiful and abundant. Did you know that God does this to us? He prunes things and people out of our lives and man it can hurt. You may feel that God has stripped you of everything; you may feel bare like my apple tree. When God wants to remove unhealthy things out of our lives, and we cling onto them, it is painful. As we hold tight, God takes His pruning shearers and snips it right out.

What are some things or people that you feel God is pruning out of your life because they are not helping you grow in your walk with Christ? What do you need to "cut" out of your life? Is it some of your music? Could it be certain movies you are watching? Maybe it is your toxic best friend that is not prodding you to love Jesus? Is it your boyfriend/girlfriend that does not really know Christ? It could even be a sibling that hinders your attempt to be clean and sober? The list could go on for miles. Trust me do not hold on to what God is trying to prune. If you truly know Christ as your Lord and Savior, you are going to want to grow in love, joy peace, patience, kindness, goodness, faithfulness, gentleness, and self-control for Him (Galatians 5).

TOUGH TO LOVE WHEN YOU FAVOR

PRUNING, DEVOTION 2
Ryan Story | *Student Pastor*

I recently made one of the hugest mistakes of my parenting career. It was one of those days at my house. My oldest son, who was almost 2, was destroying my house. He was legitimately destroying everything. Broly was taking his play hammer and pounding the walls, he took the toy hockey stick and hit several things off the wall, and somehow managed to hit his little brother Zeke. I picked up Zeke and got him to stop crying. Then I said something that I soon quickly regretted, I looked at Zeke and said, "This is why you are my favorite." Now I did not mean that wholeheartedly, but at the moment frustration got the best of me. What makes it worse was my wife heard me and came out from the kitchen and informed me why this statement was not correct to say.

Family dysfunction starts with the parents. Parents are not perfect, and kids can be hard to love, but as parents, we must stay the course and show them the example of Christ in our lives. I grew up in a family where it seemed as if it was always aunt against aunt, uncle against uncle, and cousin against cousin. It never seemed abnormal to me to be pitted against my siblings. It was never off to see my parents pitted against my aunts and uncles. Looking back on it, that kind of dysfunction can break people. Sadly, all of the drama between Jacob and Esau started with Isaac and Rebekah. Genesis 25:28 says, **"Isaac loved Esau because he ate of his game, but Rebekah loved Jacob."**

It is really easy to see how Jacob and Esau's conflict grew to split the family. It is easy to find fault in the scheming Jacob and the foolish Esau. But getting to the root of the issue shows Isaac and Rebekah's favoritism. I look at both my boys and I see the crazy, fearless Broly and I see the sweet, smiley, chunky Zeke. I love them both in different ways, but putting favor on one over the other is wrong. If we are honest, sometimes that can happen. Family life becomes difficult and tough to love when children are brought up in a world where they feel they must compete for their parent's approval.

By no means have I arrived as a parent; I am a novice at best. But I strive not to let favoritism rule in my family. We all know there are things that you like and do not like about people. Romans 2:11 says, ***"For God shows no partiality."*** God loves everyone equally; you cannot earn more or less with God. God loves you for you, not your deeds, good or bad. I took a moment where I looked at the negative actions of my son and deemed him less, and that is wrong. Isaac deemed Esau greater because he was older and a hunter. Let us let love guide our relationships with our kids, not our preference.

BAIT AND SWITCH

PRUNING, DEVOTION 3
Phil Piasecki | *Worship Leader*

There is nothing that I dislike more than being tricked. I think we have all been duped at one point or another. Maybe it was an online listing for something, but when it came in the mail it looked nothing like that ad or did not even work! My brother once ordered basketball shoes online, they came from China, and they were complete rip-offs. They were two sizes smaller than it said and looked like they could fall apart at any moment. Foolishly, I once bought a used riding lawn mower from a place with a no return policy. The ad said it started up and ran well; the only problem was that it did not do either! Sadly, we can also be tricked and deceived by people that we love, and nothing hurts more than that. I know many of us have stories that come to mind when we think about it, but I am sure none of them compare to what happened with Jacob and Rachel in Genesis chapter 29.

In this passage, we find Jacob meeting Rachel for the first time. It was love at first sight, and Jacob just knew he had to marry her. So Jacob seeks out her father, Laban, and agrees to arrange the marriage.

> Genesis 29:18-20 reads, *"**Jacob loved Rachel. And he said, 'I will serve you seven years for your younger daughter Rachel.' Laban said, 'It is better that I give her to you than that I should give her to any other man; stay with me.' So Jacob served seven years for Rachel, and they seemed to him but a few days because of the love he had for her."***

What a love story! The Scripture essentially says the seven years felt like a few days because Jacob loved Rachel so much. Unfortunately, it is at this point of the story where it all starts to fall apart.

> Genesis 29:21-27 adds, **"Then Jacob said to Laban, 'Give me my wife that I may go in to her, for my time is completed.' So Laban gathered together all the people of the place and made a feast. But in the evening he took his daughter Leah and brought her to Jacob, and he went in to her. (Laban gave his female servant Zilpah to his daughter Leah to be her servant.) And in the morning, behold, it was Leah! And Jacob said to Laban, 'What is this you have done to me? Did I not serve with you for Rachel? Why then have you deceived me?' Laban said, 'It is not so done in our country, to give the younger before the firstborn. Complete the week of this one, and we will give you the other also in return for serving me another seven years.'"**

Laban tricked Jacob and gave him his first born daughter, Leah, on their wedding night instead. Not only does he trick him, but then requires that Jacob work another seven years to marry Rachel. When we finish the story, we see that Jacob faithfully works those seven more years because he loved Rachel so much. Now, I highly doubt any of us will find ourselves in the position of Jacob and Rachel, but there is still so much that we can learn from this story to apply to our own families.

Jacob was going through a very tough time for those fourteen years, but he stayed faithful through the whole thing. He honored his commitment to Laban even though Laban did not honor his commitment. There are going to be times when family life is difficult, when being married is difficult, and when raising children is difficult, but we have to persevere because of the commitments we have made. Loving your spouse is tough sometimes, but loving them is what you committed to do. You may not always feel like loving them, but love is about a commitment, not a feeling.

Jacob committed to marry Rachel, and he worked fourteen years just to see it through! That truth needs to inspire you when you feel like giving up on the commitment that you made to your spouse. If someone told you that marriage was going to be easy, I am sorry to say that they lied to you. With Christ at the center, there can be so much joy in marriage, but there will also be hardships. There will be times when loving each other will be tough. There will be times when you are hurt, deceived, and maybe do not feel loved. We need to look at the love Jacob had for Rachel, and the love that Christ has for us, as examples of how we are to love each other. We sin against God every day, yet He still loves us unconditionally. Imitate that love and commitment in your marriage, and you will see God do incredible things.

THAT CRAZY UNCLE

PRUNING, DEVOTION 4
James Clouse | *Student Pastor*

Passage: Genesis 29:21-30

Do you have the one relative that everybody avoids during all of the family gatherings? What makes them the outcast of the party? Why does everybody avoid that person? It is possible that the person may have caused a bunch of trouble in the past and is now kind of the outcast of the party.

While it is good to make sure we forgive people of their past and move on, we also should be careful of family members that have a bad reputation. There are instances where I may be careful which relatives I let watch my daughter or to which relatives I lend money.

Jacob also had an uncle that was not worthy of his trust.

> *"Then Jacob said to Laban, 'Give me my wife that I may go in to her, for my time is completed.' So Laban gathered together all the people of the place and made a feast. But in the evening he took his daughter Leah and brought her to Jacob, and he went in to her."*

> *"And in the morning, behold, it was Leah! And Jacob said to Laban, 'What is this you have done to me? Did I not serve with you for Rachel? Why then have you deceived me?' Laban said, 'It is not so done in our country, to give the younger before the firstborn. Complete the week of this one, and we will give you the other also in return for serving me another seven years.' Jacob did so, and completed her week. Then Laban gave him his daughter Rachel to be his wife."*

PRUNING DEVOTION 4

> *"So Jacob went in to Rachel also, and he loved Rachel more than Leah, and served Laban for another seven years."*
> *(Genesis 29:21-23, 25-28, 30)*

To give some context here, Jacob was sent to find a wife from his family. So Jacob went on a journey to find a wife (not so different from now). As Rachel, a shepherdess was coming to water her sheep Jacob noticed her. He showed off his muscle and won her over.

Jacob then spoke with Laban, her father, saying he wanted to marry her. Laban agreed but with a price; Jacob was to work for him for seven years. Jacob did so without any argument. The day of the wedding Laban gave him the wrong wife (talk about crazy!). I am sure that Laban could have told Jacob that Leah had to be married first before Rachel, but instead, he chose to take advantage of Jacob.

But instead of arguing with Jacob and going after him with a vengeance, Jacob did what he needed to do to marry Rachel, the one whom he loved.

We can learn from Jacob when it comes to our relatives who are hard to deal with or cause problems. We need to learn to forgive, but also be cautious of them. I am sure that Jacob thought twice in the future before letting Laban get too close to his family.

FORGIVENESS

PRUNING, DEVOTION 5
Richie Henson | *Production Director*

I have always loved the quote from the late Rear Admiral Grace Murray Hopper, "It is easier to ask forgiveness than it is to get permission." As a young man, I often used this quote to justify all sorts of foolish activity such as racing shopping carts and riding our bikes to go to get slushies at midnight. However, as I get older, and experience greater maturity, I realize how difficult it is to truly ask for forgiveness. It is not simply to say I am sorry, but to express my understanding of how I have wronged another and to attempt to make amends through humility.

This concept of true forgiveness has proven to be one of the more difficult hurdles in my family life. As a teenager, I became consumed with grudges and anger towards those who wronged me. I felt that justice was required for every offense both big and small. This poor attitude and perspective also found its way into my early marriage. It is truly a stumbling block that I must continually give to Jesus to overcome.

In the story of Jacob, beginning in Genesis chapter 32, we see that Jacob is asked by God to return to his homeland thereby putting him in direct contact with his estranged brother Esau. Jacob toils with the choice of facing his brother whom he has greatly wronged and eventually gives in to the will of God and goes to confront Esau. In my mind, this would be a perfect place in the story for Esau to unleash the rage of years gone by and exact justice against Jacob.

However, Genesis 33:1-4 tells us, "And Jacob lifted up his eyes and looked, and behold, Esau was coming, and four hundred men with him. So he divided the children among Leah and Rachel and the two female servants. And he put the servants with their children in front, then Leah with her children, and Rachel and Joseph last of all. He himself went on before them, bowing himself to the ground seven times, until he came near to his brother. But Esau ran to meet him and embraced him and fell on his neck and kissed him, and they wept."

What a beautiful scene depicted for us here. Two brothers torn apart by their past are reunited. Jacob is distraught by his past actions and knows Esau has every right to be angry, but Esau has taken the time to deal with the grief of Jacob stealing his birth right and he can embrace his brother in forgiveness.

We, as Christians, have all experienced a similar moment of total forgiveness. When we accept Jesus as our Lord and Savior, God's forgiveness comes freely and immediately. Although we are broken over our wrong doing, God shows nothing but forgiveness. It is my hope that as we continue to grow in the understanding of God's forgiveness of our sins, we will be able to extend and teach our families the same kind of generous forgiveness that Esau expresses here.

DISCIPLINE

PRUNING, DEVOTION 6
Jeff England | *Counseling Pastor*

"God does not discipline us to subdue us, but to condition us for a life of usefulness and blessedness." Billy Graham

We have all watched the scene play out. Maybe in a restaurant, maybe a store, maybe at someone's home or in your own house, when that child goes wild. That out of control, seemingly spoiled rotten, ill-tempered "brat" unwinds! How quick we are to rush to judgments saying or thinking, "They better get that one under control," "You know what would happen to that one if he was mine," or "Someone better start learning how to parent." It is true that undisciplined children learn quickly how to get what they want and may go to crazy extremes to convince their authorities to say "OK." I have counseled long enough to know, however, that even the most skilled parents have children that test the limits and act out. I love the quiet confidence of that mom or dad who knows exactly what to do when their little one hits the floor in the middle of a store in a calculated rage. They leave the cart, take the swift removal of the child, and have some "fellowship" back in the car or at home. That child will learn to behave appropriately. Not only do they learn to respect authority and rules but they grow more secure, confident, and the seeds for understanding God's plan of discipline are sown.

> ***"My son, do not despise the LORD'S discipline or be weary of his reproof, for the LORD reproves him who he loves, as a father the son in whom he delights."*** Proverbs 3:11-12

As a parent, we know that it is sometimes so much easier to give in to the demands of that child whose fury is building. I cannot tell you how many times I have helped a parent develop a plan for disciplining their child and then that parent has ended up telling me that the plan was too hard or the plan seemed to punish them as the parent. Discipline takes time, energy, patience, perseverance, and yes, sacrifice! But discipline is truly an act of love. Proverbs 13:24 makes it clear, **"Whoever spares the rod hates his son, but he who loves him is diligent to discipline him."** No one likes to be disciplined, but I find great comfort in the fact that as a child of God, He loves me enough to patiently correct me when I stray. From His example, we are taught how to care for our children.

Proverbs 6:23 gives more insight into why correcting our children is so very important. **"For the commandment is a lamp and the teaching a light, and the reproofs of discipline are the way of life."** Have you ever watched a sunrise from the shores of the Atlantic Ocean or the heights of a mountain? Beyond the beauty of those moments is the promise of another day filled with light that allows us to more easily navigate our way through the snares and pitfalls of the world. Godly discipline illuminates our children's lives in a similar manner. When a young person has been taught biblical right from wrong, it is as if you have given your child an endless supply of lamps. Each time they are confronted by the darkness of worldly desires, they need only refer back to one of your lessons – or turn on a lamp. When we have sown the Word of God in our hearts and passed it along to our children, the light of God's way can help them avoid many struggles. Finally, when our children choose God over the world in their daily lives, no sunrise will ever match the beauty of their growth!

I hope patient, loving correction with a desire to keep your children from going astray is your method and goal. Proverbs 19:18 says, **"Discipline your son, for there is hope; do not set your heart on putting him to death."** I am not only thankful that God corrects his children, but I am thankful that he disciplines with love and control. The parent that lashes out in fits of rage when upset with their child often makes choices that do not teach or demonstrate love but may build a wall of resentment between parent and child that can destroy trust and create long term separation. In Proverbs 29:17, Solomon reminds us of the importance and benefits of godly discipline with our children, **"Discipline your son, and he will give you rest; he will give delight to your heart."**

My wife and I have been privileged to teach four and five-year-olds during the gathering for the past 14 years. I have not only been delighted by my daughters when they have made great choices, but I feel that same sense of joy when I witness our students demonstrate random acts of kindness, patience, and obedience. The sense of peace we feel as parents when our children consistently make good choices is wonderful.

A final word from Proverbs on the importance of correcting our children is found in Chapter 5 verse 23, **"He dies for lack of discipline, and because of his great folly he is led astray."**

I hope you have an incredible day as you ponder the nature of godly discipline. You can do this. Set the godly example of a disciplined life then teach your children to follow it.

04
BLOOMING

DR. RANDY T. JOHNSON,
GROWTH PASTOR

BLOOMING WEEK 4

My father-in-law, Sam, loves his garden. Even though he lives in Sterling Heights, he has a large garden. I remember when I was dating my wife, Angela. As I came to their house, he was either sitting on the porch or "playing" in his garden.

He grows strawberries, raspberries, onions, cucumbers, squash, green beans, asparagus, tomatoes, and even kohlrabi. He is over ninety years old and still brings us fresh treats from his garden each week all summer long.

Were you raised with a garden or have one now? *flowers not fruits/veggies until I had kids*

He loves to share the fruit of his labor with others. He does not need a garden. He can afford to buy any necessary groceries, but he has his reasons. First, he likes to do things on his own. He likes growing his food. Nothing tastes as good as his garden delicacies. He is from Virginia, and I guess it is true, "you can take a boy out of the country, but you cannot take the country out of the boy." Second, he likes to share his crop with others. One of his love languages must be gifts because he is regularly handing friends and family fresh produce.

What other skills can be used to bless others? *any that you have*

The Fruit of the Spirit is our garden. What is born out of a life changing knowledge (the Gospel) can rescue people and change them. If they see our **"love, joy, peace, patience, kindness, goodness, faithfulness, gentleness, and self-control"** (Galatians 5:22-23), they will see a difference, something that speaks to something greater in our lives. Only true fruit will show that, and only <u>true fruit will come from a life changed by God.</u>

79

BLOOMING WEEK 4

Which of those character traits comes most naturally for you? *None - Kindness? loving?*

Which trait challenges you the most? *all of them*

Please realize it is the Fruit, not fruits, of the Spirit. We need all nine aspects of this fruit in our lives. However, it is still good to focus and work on each trait individually. The Fruit of the Spirit has been generalized in today's culture, do we know what they each mean? Have we thought about what they look like in the reality of our lives? It is important to take a look at each of them.

1. Love *and now abide faith hope, love these 3 but the greatest love.*

Do you think there is a reason for the order of these traits (1 Corinthians 13:13)? *With abiding faith comes hope love.*

> "A new commandment I give to you, that you love one another: just as I have loved you, you also are to love one another. By this all people will know that you are my disciples, if you have love for one another" (John 13:34-35).

Summarize this verse in five words or less. *love all as God loves*

BLOOMING WEEK 4

"If we don't have the Word of God as the foundation of what we believe, we will have a faulty footing—it will not stand against the elements that will come against us. God has designed both our physical and spiritual lives to be ordered by one key attribute upon which the fruit of the Spirit is based—that foundation is love."
- David Jeremiah

How can love be created, developed, or strengthened? _?_
ask Wisdom,

2. Joy

> *"Count it all joy, my brothers, when you meet trials of various kinds, for you know that the testing of your faith produces steadfastness"* (James 1:2-3).

How is joy different from happiness? _feelings ✓ external things_
make peace with who you are, why you are & how you are.

Billy Sunday has said, "If you have no joy, there's a leak in your Christianity somewhere."

What does he mean? _your peace in faith has hole, relook at yourself._

3. Peace

> Philippians 4:7 says, *"And the peace of God, which surpasses all understanding, will guard your hearts and your minds in Christ Jesus."*

BLOOMING WEEK 4

What does this verse mean? *God peace guards everything*

"Cultivate peace and harmony with all." - George Washington

How important is peace? Is it always possible? *If all believe its possible, it is important*

Romans 12:18

4. Patience

Isiah 4

Genesis 29:20 says, *"So Jacob served seven years for Rachel, and they seemed to him but a few days because of the love he had for her."*

Explain the story of this verse. How can it relate to us? *Love makes time fly easily*

"Genius is eternal patience." – Michelangelo

What did he mean? *Wisdom guides faith & patience*

5. Kindness

Proverbs 19:22 (NASB) describes kindness as making one good-looking, *"What is desirable in a man is his kindness, And it is better to be a poor man than a liar."*

How does kindness make one more attractive? _____
opens the heart to love

Henry Drummond, Scottish Evangelist, said, "Have you ever noticed how much of Christ's life was spent in doing kind things?"

What were some kind things Jesus did? _____
gave life our sins

6. Goodness

Galatians 6:10 says, **"So then, as we have opportunity, let us do good to everyone, and especially to those who are of the household of faith."**

How should we apply this verse? *Do good to all + more good to church (serve)*

"True religion is real living; living with all one's soul, with all one's goodness and righteousness." - Albert Einstein

Since we are not saved by works, why be good? _____
god has plan, its to be good.

7. Faithfulness

Hebrews 12:1 says, *"Therefore, since we are surrounded by so great a cloud of witnesses, let us also lay aside every weight, and sin which clings so closely, and let us run with endurance the race that is set before us."*

What does faithfulness mean? _____

"Many Christians estimate difficulty in the light of their own resources, and thus they attempt very little and they always fail. All giants have been weak men who did great things for God because they reckoned on His power and presence to be with them." - James Hudson Taylor

What is God calling you to do that is bigger than you? _____
pray - help others
grow - church

8. Gentleness

Philippians 4:5 (NIV) says, *"Let your gentleness be evident to all. The Lord is near."* It is interesting to see what words other translations use for the word "gentleness:" moderation (KJV), gentle spirit (NASB), reasonableness (ESV), and gentleness (NKJV). The Amplified Bible says it this way, *"Let your gentle spirit [your graciousness, unselfishness, mercy, tolerance, and patience] be known to all people. The Lord is near."*

BLOOMING WEEK 4

How would you define gentleness? _kind / mild mannered_

It has been said, "Nothing is so strong as gentleness, nothing so gentle as real strength."
Do you agree or disagree? _?_

9. Self-control

> 1 Corinthians 10:13 says, *"No temptation has overtaken you that is not common to man. God is faithful, and he will not let you be tempted beyond your ability, but with the temptation he will also provide the way of escape, that you may be able to endure it."*

How does this verse relate to self-control? _not tempted past our ability_

"If you lose self-control everything will fall." - John Wooden

What does this mean? _everything will fall_

> Matthew 7:16-20 says, *"You will recognize them by their fruits. Are grapes gathered from thornbushes, or figs from thistles? So, every healthy tree bears good fruit, but the diseased tree bears bad fruit. A healthy tree cannot bear*

bad fruit, nor can a diseased tree bear good fruit. Every tree that does not bear good fruit is cut down and thrown into the fire. Thus you will recognize them by their fruits."

How do or should people recognize Christians? *With all the abiding attributes faith, kind, etc...*

What do you need to do better? *All of it pray / faithfulness*

"It is of no use for any of you to try to be soul-winners if you are not bearing fruit in your own lives. How can you serve the Lord with your lips if you do not serve Him with your lives? How can you preach His gospel with your tongues, when with hands, feet, and heart you are preaching the devil's gospel, and setting up an antichrist by your practical unholiness?" - Charles Spurgeon

LOVE

BLOOMING, DEVOTION 1
Katrina Young | *Nursery and Pre-K Director*

"Remain in me, as I also remain in you. No branch can bear fruit by itself; it must remain in the vine. Neither can you bear fruit unless you remain in me." John 15:4 (NIV)

There is a new craze going on in my family researching our family tree. Some have purchased DNA testing kits to find their ancestry and heritage. It is interesting how easy it is to research someone that lived many years ago. Like putting a puzzle together connecting the dots of lineage, there is a sense of accomplishment finding the missing piece, but there is no real connection to the person, no emotional or spiritual bond, just a name, a year of birth or death that connects them to you. Sadly, this is true in families today, the root of the family tree has withered, some of the branches are broken, and there is no source of love from which to draw.

What does real love look like?

"Love is patient and kind; love does not envy or boast; it is not arrogant or rude. It does not insist on its own way; it is not irritable or resentful; it does not rejoice at wrongdoing, but rejoices with the truth. Love bears all things, believes all things, hopes all things, endures all things." 1 Corinthians 13:4-7

As Christians, we are called to love, *"This is my commandment, that you love one another as I have loved you"* (John 15:12). It was not until I became a Christian that I began to understand these verses. As I grew in Christ, it became clearer how to not only accept love but to also love others. Loving the way God loves us requires understanding how much He loves us. God's love is unconditional; learning to love in that way is a walk through patience, forgiveness, and sacrifice.

The love that I have for my kids is beyond measure; there is nothing that I would not do for them. It is within our families first that we begin to understand what unconditional love is, and it is often the ones that are closest to us that can bring the biggest challenge. We, like any other family, have gone through many difficult times. Keeping Christ in the center of those situations enabled us to grow as a family and deeper in our walk.

As believers, we are a new creation; our identity is not in a family tree that extends back centuries and has many branches; it is in Him. When we lean on, trust in, and rely on His word and His ways we strengthen our family and relationships. It is then that we can experience the Fruit of the Spirit.

"But the fruit of the Spirit is love, joy, peace, patience, kindness, goodness, faithfulness, gentleness, self-control; against such things there is no law" (Galatians 5:22-23).

JOY

BLOOMING, DEVOTION 2
Tommy Youngquist | *Children's Pastor*

I Believe God's Promises

Walk in the Spirit!? How in the world do I do that? I have asked this question multiple times. I am sure you have, too. Paul tells us in Galatians 5:16 (KJV) to ***"Walk in the Spirit."*** Then he goes on to list all of the things our flesh wants to walk in like drunkenness, sexual immorality, and anger. You know, sin. After listing our fleshly sins, he lists nine things to help us combat those sins and ***"Walk in the Spirit."*** I would specifically like to address joy.

A simple definition of joy is believing God's promises. Now, it is easy to believe God's promises when the bills are paid, no major health issues are happening in the family, and everyone is happy and worry-free. However, what about believing in God when something horrible happens? Take Paul, for example, a man who lost his sight for a while, was constantly put in prison, beaten, ridiculed, and lonely, but said, ***"In all my affliction, I am overflowing with joy"*** (2 Corinthians 7:4). Where did he find this incredibly durable joy?

It came from simply believing (with all of his heart) that God's promises are true. Jesus taught us in the Gospels that the storms of life will happen. Translation: bad things happen, even to good people. Paul's joy came from something beyond his momentary circumstances. True joy comes from knowing what Jesus did for you and trusting in Him to fulfill His promises to you. So what are His promises?

- Salvation to all who believe in Jesus (Romans 1:16-17)
- Everything will work out for good for His children (Romans 8:28)
- Comfort in trials (1 Corinthians 1:3-4)
- Peace when we pray (Philippians 4:6-7)
- Supplying all of our needs (Matthew 6:33)

I could go on and on. You could read many, many more promises in the Bible. The choice you need to make is are you going to believe (with all your heart) God's promises. If you choose to believe, your joy does not change when things do not go your way because you trust God no matter the circumstance.

PEACE

BLOOMING, DEVOTION 3
James Mann | *Children's Director*

The Lord's Covenant of Peace

"I will make with them a covenant of peace and banish wild beasts from the land, so that they may dwell securely in the wilderness and sleep in the woods. And I will make them and the places all around my hill a blessing, and I will send down the showers in their season; they shall be showers of blessing. And the trees of the field shall yield their fruit, and the earth shall yield its increase, and they shall be secure in their land. And they shall know that I am the LORD, when I break the bars of their yoke, and deliver them from the hand of those who enslaved them." Ezekiel 34:25-27

Peace is an interesting topic to study in the Bible. There are many different types of peace that are discussed throughout Scripture. The most important peace to look into is the peace you find in the Lord. Many people are searching for peace in their family's lives in the wrong places. Mankind teaches us that peace goes hand-in-hand with money and stability. This leads to a false sense of peace that is soon corrupted and then destroyed because it exists without the Lord.

Peace should be searched for and found in Christ Jesus. By reading the passage in Ezekiel, we learn about the Lord getting rid of the wild beasts, which I would like to think of like the sin of the world so that you can sleep securely in the wilderness. As a family, if you find peace in the wilderness, then you will be able to live securely and peacefully. Then Ezekiel goes to explain even further and say,

BLOOMING DEVOTION 3

"And the trees of the field shall yield their fruit, and the earth shall yield its increase, and they shall be secure in their land." To yield fruit, and then increase, is only accomplished through finding your peace in the Lord.

So you may be asking yourself now, "How can my family find peace in the Lord?" This is a difficult, but rewarding path to take. To find peace in the Lord is to leave behind the things of life that only satisfy momentarily. You must turn to the Bread of Life, who makes it so you never hunger again. In case you are wondering what this bread is, it is Jesus who put His life down for you. Only then will you be satisfied as a family, and only then will you find peace in the family.

PATIENCE

BLOOMING, DEVOTION 4
Mark O'Connor | *Student Director*

I just got back from two weeks of student summer camps. I had to laugh a bit as I began to type this devotion on patience. My patience was tested more in one week of middle school camp than it had been in the last couple years of serving in student ministry. It has always been a little odd how patience has worked in my life. When it comes to people, I have never had a problem. However, this week of middle school camp was a problem for me. There were three kids that took the vast majority of my time from the rest of the students from our location. Those that know me well know that I am the slowest person to anger or freak out in the history of the world. There was one situation though that I observed a particularly awful piece of behavior that I finally lost my cool. Rightfully so as I was defending a student, I lost all chill. At that moment though, I recognized that I needed to handle the situation with the grace and patience I have been afforded so many times in my life. I had to retreat for a moment, and this Scripture popped into my mind:

> Ecclesiastes 7:9 says, ***"Be not quick in your spirit to become angry, for anger lodges in the heart of fools."***

I had lost sight of a principle I held very dear to me. At that moment, the enemy had placed a wedge between Jesus and me. All evidence of the Fruit of the Spirit had left my mind and body. It is easy for us to let that happen. Maybe you are a parent with a child that has challenging behaviors. Maybe you are teen struggling with your parent's authority. We need to rely on the Holy Spirit in those times to carry us through the challenge. It is very easy for us to think we can do it on our own. We live like that until something blows our world up, and it is in those moments that we surrender completely to the will of God and realize that He will carry us through whatever circumstance comes into our life. That is, as long as we rely not on our knowledge and understanding but His.

KINDNESS

BLOOMING, DEVOTION 5
Max Sinclair | *Children's Director*

Whenever I read Galatians, and I get to the portion where Paul lists off the Fruit of the Spirit, I always read through and think of the individual attributes of the fruit. One of them that I honestly have a hard time grasping is kindness. I was raised in a good home and full of love and the love of Christ, but one thing that my mother would always say is that we need to be kind. Of all the traits, she focused on kindness. It must be important. However, to this date, I struggle with the idea of what kindness truly is.

As I read in the Bible, for instances of kindness, it drips off the pages. One example in the Old Testament is the story of Mephibosheth. He was Saul's grandson. Saul, who was trying to kill David, died. Instead of taking revenge, David receives Mephibosheth at his table. He shows amazing kindness. Obviously, the greatest example of kindness was shown when Jesus died on the cross for our sin.

Instead of elaborating on a story and trying to gain knowledge from it, or read a large passage of Scripture to try to aid me in this topic, I will just give you the words of Christ from Luke chapter 6:34-36, *"And if you lend to those from whom you expect to receive, what credit is that to you? Even sinners lend to sinners, to get back the same amount. But love your enemies, and do good, and lend, expecting nothing in return, and your reward will be great, and you will be sons of the Most High, for he is kind to the ungrateful and the evil. Be merciful, even as your Father is merciful."*

This Scripture is quite poignant in the fact that Jesus tells us that we are to be kind to all, from sinners to our enemies. So now the question is, how does this apply to the family? Too often, we are kind all day and stop when we get home. We should be kind to strangers, but the fact remains, we need to be kind to our families. I am not a parent, so the only thing I can say about parenting is from a child's point of view, but kindness should not be absent from it. When dealing with a problem remember to be kind, but at the same time, one needs to maintain integrity and firmness. Kindness is very important; it shows the love not only we have for our children, but the love that Christ showed to us.

GOODNESS

BLOOMING, DEVOTION 6
Kyle Wendel | *Children and Student's Director*

I do not know about you guys, but I cannot think about the Fruit of the Spirit without thinking of the children's song about them. Maybe that is because I am one of the Children's Directors, who knows. To this day it is honestly how I remember the fruit. If you have not heard the song yet, you need to go to YouTube "Fruit of the Spirit song." You will not regret it.

> *"Ohhhhhh the fruit of the Spirit's not a coconut*
> *The Fruit of the Spirit's not a coconut*
> *If you want to be a coconut*
> *You might as well hear it:*
> *You can't be a fruit of the Spirit.*
>
> *Cause the fruit is*
> *Love, joy, peace, patience,*
> *Kindness, goodness, faithfulness*
> *Gentleness and self-control."*

Today we are going to talking about the Fruit of the Spirit called goodness. Goodness means working for the benefit of others, not oneself. If we take a look at Galatians 6:10 it also mentions what goodness should look like in us.

> *"So then, as we have opportunity, let us do good to everyone, and especially to those who are of the household of faith."*

As followers of Christ, we should always be looking to have the Fruit of the Spirit in our lives. The Bible tells us that a good tree bears fruit. As Christians, we should be able to see the fruit in our lives. We should see this fruit growing over time in our lives. If this fruit is not evident in our lives, there needs to be some serious reflection. A tree that is not bearing fruit is a dead tree. Dead trees get cut down. We do not want to be walking around like a dead tree without fruit. Instead, a fruit we need to have is goodness.

The Bible says that every opportunity we have to do good we should do it. Man, we have a lot of opportunities! The verse also goes on to say especially do good to those of the faith. We need to constantly be looking for opportunities in our lives to do good to others. One, because it can show the Gospel to the unbeliever and two because it is a way to worship our Lord. We know the good that He has done to us. We should just be so grateful that we should always be looking for ways to do good to others. Let that fruit start to blossom in your life! Let us stop looking at what we can do to benefit ourselves and look how we can benefit others.

FAITHFULNESS

BLOOMING, DEVOTION 7
Ryan Story | *Student Pastor*

The Jump

"Dad's beard is sweet."
"One, Two,... What comes after two?"
"Ball?"
"I am going to jump now!"
"Pool time."

These are thoughts I imagine running through my son's head at his swim class. My wife and I felt it would be wise to enroll our son in swim classes before the summer began in hopes to teach him the basics of swimming. On one particular day, the instructor wanted us to work with our children to make sure they understood not to jump in unless a parent was present and wanting them to jump. Several times I set Broly on the ledge and counted to three. More than once Broly could not wait until the end of two before he jumped into the pool. This became frustrating and cute all in one. In hopes my son would understand the importance of making sure it was safe, I started to take steps further away from him. In my mind, I figured Broly would not want to jump in with me being out of arms distance. Yeah, that did not work. He still would jump in the pool, and I would have to take a quick stride to make sure he was safe. While I enjoy my son's tenacity and fearlessness, this was not one of those times. I kept repeating the same pattern, but he always seemed to jump early. On our way home, it dawned on me, Broly's fearlessness was not due to the lack of fear, his fearlessness was because he had complete faith that his father would be there to help.

In the short amount of time I have been a father, I feel I have learned so much about God. I sit, and I watch my interactions with my sons, and I seem to find moments in the Bible that coincide. When my sons look at me, I hope, there is never a moment that they are hesitant to trust me. Their faithfulness of believing their father is there for them is truly inspirational. My son would jump into a pool without the slightest degree of fear because he knew his father was too faithful to let him drop and fail. I stopped and scrolled through the Bible today and started thinking about how faithful God has been to us.

- God showed His faithfulness to save Noah and his family from the flood.
- God showed faithfulness to fulfill His promises to Abraham and created a great nation.
- God's faithfulness was still evident to the children of Israel while they were in Egypt and wandering in the wilderness.
- God's faithfulness made a shepherd boy into a great king.
- God's faithfulness is even demonstrated in the failures of the Israelites when they are taken into exile and brought them back to the land He promised long ago.
- God's faithfulness even sent His son to die on a cross for our sins.
- God's faithfulness has Him present even in our worst failures. He is there to redeem, restore and re-strengthen us.

There was never a moment of doubt in my son's mind when it came to putting his faith in me to catch him at the pool. He walked up to the edge and just jumped in. There was no "what if he is not there" or "what if my face gets wet." There was complete trust and faith in his father. Imagine if our walk with God was like that. Imagine if we trusted God so much we were willing to step to the edge and just jump completely into His arms. What could happen if we gave God our 100%? We can trust Him to the point that we would live how He intended. Imagine if we all tried to reproduce this faithfulness in our families. Imagine if children had so much faith in their parents, they never had to question if their parents were proud of them. Imagine if a wife never had to doubt that she was still the one person her husband cherished above every other person. Imagine if a husband had the faith to lead his family where God wanted his family and that his family would follow. Sometimes in life, we just have to jump knowing God will catch us.

GENTLENESS

BLOOMING, DEVOTION 8
Phil Piasecki | *Worship Leader*

I once had a Pastor tell me that every morning he prays and asks the Holy Spirit to guide his "thoughts, actions, and reactions." The idea of praying for my thoughts and actions to be guided by God was something that I had understood and regularly done, but the idea of praying about my reactions was something that had never crossed my mind. When we stop and think about it, so much of our lives are spent reacting to things. This has become even more evident in my life since being married and having a child. Within the family, we are constantly reacting to each other. How we react speaks deeply to the spiritual health of the family. A family that is rooted in Jesus Christ will react in a way that reflects the Fruit of the Spirit.

> Proverbs 15:1 says, **"A soft answer turns away wrath, but a harsh word stirs up anger."**

If our family tree is blooming and producing fruit, our reactions will be filled with gentleness. We all can think of examples in our lives when we have to choose how we are going to respond, with gentleness or with wrath. Proverbs 15:1 is such a simple and powerful Scripture. We all know it to be true, when we respond with gentleness it can diffuse a situation, or we can respond with harsh words and stir up anger. Husbands and wives know this better than anyone, in the midst of a fight there is that point where you can decide how to respond. We all know that the harsh response is only going to lead to more anger, yet so many of us still choose it! The next time your spouse, child, or parent gets angry with you, choose to respond in gentleness. I promise that you will see an incredible difference begin in the spiritual health of your family! Fights between family members will be shorter or not even happen in the first place. However, this cannot happen by your power. None of us on our own have the power to respond with gentleness. We need the power of the Holy Spirit to strengthen us to reflect Christ every day. Start your day off as a family in prayer asking Christ to give you the power to respond in gentleness. Pray asking the Holy Spirit to guide your thoughts, actions, and reactions. A family that responds in gentleness is a family producing the Fruit of the Spirit and reflecting the character of Christ.

SELF-CONTROL

BLOOMING, DEVOTION 9
Donna Fox | *Assistant to the Growth Pastor*

"But the fruit of the Spirit is love, joy, peace, patience, kindness, goodness, faithfulness, gentleness, self-control; against such things there is no law." Galatians 5:22-23

What is self-control? If there's a candy bar on your desk, do you pick it up and eat it without thinking first? (Note: I speak from experience here!) If someone angers you, do you fly off the handle? Self-control, according to the Merriam Webster Dictionary, is having control over your feelings or actions. Wikipedia goes further to explain that self-control is the ability to regulate one's emotions, thoughts, and behavior in the face of temptations and impulses.

There are several examples of people exhibiting self-control in the Bible, from Joseph to Job to Jesus, and several examples of people not exhibiting self-control, from Eve to Samson (and on and on!). But how do you obtain self-control? It begins at the time of salvation, and it grows or becomes more apparent, and as you mature in your Christianity. The Holy Spirit, being in the Word, and learning through a Growth Community lesson, will all help you learn right from wrong, good from evil. You will conscientiously begin to make different decisions based on this new found knowledge. You will begin to THINK before you ACT and decide – do I need to eat that candy bar or this apple? Do I need to go into that bar or should I keep driving? Should I yell in anger, or count to 10 and calm down first? You will begin to exercise self-control to avoid temptations. When you know that you can do something that is not good for you, but do not, that is self-control!

The Fruit of the Spirit in Galatians 5:22-23 is from the Holy Spirit. Galatians 5:16-17 says, *"But I say, walk by the Spirit, and you will not gratify the desires of the flesh. For the desires of the flesh are against the Spirit, and the desires of the Spirit are against the flesh, for these are opposed to each other, to keep you from doing the things you want to do."* Worldly things tempt us, but we have free will to decide as to what to do when faced with that temptation. Do we give in to our worldly desire, or do we exercise self-control?

The first step is to control our thoughts. By controlling our thoughts, we can then control our actions. 2 Corinthians 10:5 says, *"Take every thought captive to obey Christ."* As soon as a negative or bad thought creeps in, think of something else. Philippians 4:8 gives a nice list, *"Finally, brothers, whatever is true, whatever is honorable, whatever is just, whatever is pure, whatever is lovely, whatever is commendable, if there is any excellence, if there is anything worthy of praise, think about these things."*

Another way to gain self-control is to avoid temptations. Luke 22:40 reads, *"Pray that you may not enter into temptation."* 1 Corinthians 10:13 adds, *"No temptation has overtaken you that is not common to man. God is faithful, and he will not let you be tempted beyond your ability, but with the temptation he will also provide the way of escape, that you may be able to endure it."*

Lastly, we all make mistakes. Forgive yourself and move forward. The prophet Jeremiah, in verse 31:34 says, *"For I will forgive their iniquity, and I will remember their sin no more."* If Jesus forgives your iniquities, should you not also forgive yourself for your loss of self-control? Start again fresh each hour, each day, and let the Holy Spirit guide you in your thoughts and actions.

"What lies in our power to do, lies in our power not to do." - Aristotle

OUR MISSION

Matthew 28:19-20: *"Go therefore and make disciples of all nations, baptizing them in the name of the Father and of the Son and of the Holy Spirit, teaching them to observe all that I have commanded you. And behold, I am with you always, to the end of the age."*

REACH

At The River Church, you will often hear the phrase, "we don't go to church, we are the Church." We believe that as God's people, our primary purpose and goal is to go out and make disciples of Jesus Christ. We encourage you to reach the world in your local communities.

GATHER

Weekend Gatherings at The River Church are all about Jesus, through singing, giving, serving, baptizing, taking the Lord's Supper, and participating in messages that are all about Jesus and bringing glory to Him. We know that when followers of Christ gather together in unity, it's not only a refresher it's bringing life-change.

GROW

Our Growth Communities are designed to mirror the early church in Acts as having "all things in common." They are smaller collections of believers who spend time together studying the word, knowing and caring for one another relationally, and learning to increase their commitment to Christ by holding one another accountable.

The River Church
8393 E. Holly Rd. Holly, MI 48442
theriverchurch.cc • info@theriverchurch.cc

BOOKS BY THE RIVER CHURCH

life ins.

$28 - 50,000 me (29)
   15 yr.

$72 30 year 200,000 (52)

Tobacco free 1 year